50 NIFTY

Cartoon Characters

TO

DRAW

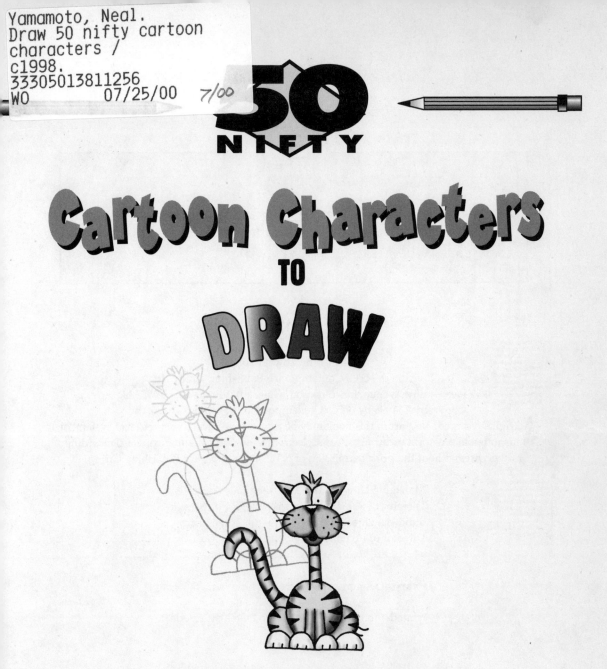

Illustrated by Neal Yamamoto
Text by Amy Margaret

NOTE: The numbered eraser in the upper right-hand corner of each project indicates the level of difficulty—1 being the easiest and 3 the hardest.

Published by Lowell House
A division of NTC/Contemporary Publishing Group, Inc.
4255 West Touhy Avenue, Lincolnwood (Chicago), Illinois 60646-1975 U.S.A.
Copyright © 1998 by NTC/Contemporary Publishing Group, Inc.

Managing Director and Publisher: Jack Artenstein
Director of Publishing Services: Rena Copperman
Editorial Director, Juvenile: Brenda Pope-Ostrow
Director of Juvenile Development: Amy Downing
Director of Art Production: Bret Perry

Library of Congress Catalog Card Number: 98-66656
ISBN: 0-7373-0035-3
Printed and bound in the United States of America

10   9   8   7   6   5   4

Lowell House books can be purchased at special discounts
when ordered in bulk for premiums and special sales.
Contact Customer Service at the following address:
4255 West Touhy Avenue, Lincolnwood (Chicago), Illinois 60646-1975 U.S.A.
1-800-323-4900

Contents

Monkey Face

DRAW THIS SILLY MONKEY FOR ONE OF YOUR BUDDIES WHO LIKES TO JUST HANG AROUND!

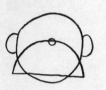

1. First sketch a circle for the monkey's head. Then add a large half-circle for its mouth area. Draw its nose and two ears.

2. Above its nose, add two large eyes. Then, below the head, sketch a circle for its belly.

3. Draw the monkey's arms, legs, and neck.

4. Add round shapes for its hands and feet. Sketch a smaller circle inside its belly.

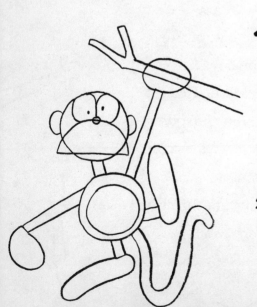

5. Add two tiny pupils in the monkey's eyes, a tail, and a twig the monkey can dangle from.

6. Sketch the monkey's fingers—monkeys have opposable thumbs just like you! Draw fur lines along its wrists.

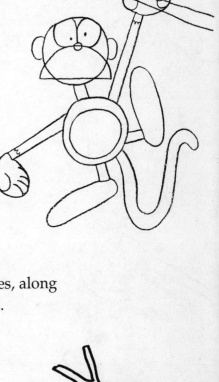

7. Now add the monkey's toes, along with fur lines on its ankles.

8. Further shape the toes and fingers, and erase all unnecessary lines. For the finishing touches, draw the nose and eyebrows. Add details to the ears.

Cry, Baby, Cry!

NOW, THIS IS ONE CHARACTER THAT'S MORE FUN ON PAPER THAN IN REAL LIFE!

1. Draw two large circles, one on top of the other. Then draw a slightly smaller circle inside the top circle. Begin to create the feet with two small circles at the base of the bottom circle.

2. Add three partial circles on the top circle, its head. These shapes will be the baby's nose and ears. Sketch two arm shapes.

3. Begin to add details, such as the nostrils, a single large tooth, and two round shapes for the hands. Don't forget to add the fat baby toes!

4. Now draw the stubby digits on the baby's hands, as well as a diaper around its lower half.

5. Erase all unneeded lines. Color in the baby's open mouth and eyes, which are squirting out tears. Detai the diaper, and add the belly button. Finally, draw th curved motion lines around the hands.

6

Funny Fish

OM THE OCEAN BLUE COMES THIS FAR-OUT FISHIE. IT'S SO EASY TO MAKE YOU MAY WANT TO CREATE A WHOLE SCHOOL!

1. Create the eye-shaped body of the fish.

2. Add its three fins. Draw the fish's large eyes and silly grin.

3. Dot the fish's eyes with small pupils, and add a curved line to suggest its gills.

4. Erase extra lines in the fins and eyes. Last, add scales and tiny bubbles.

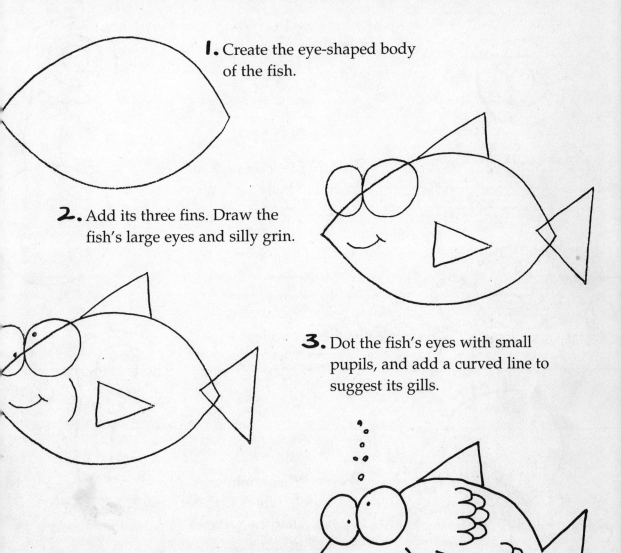

Got My Eye on You

3

THIS SWEET LITTLE ALIEN COULDN'T HURT AN ANT. SHE FALLS IN LOVE WITH EVERYONE SHE MEETS!

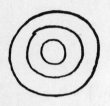

1. Draw three circles, one inside the other.

2. Add her long neck and round belly.

3. Create the alien's two legs.

4. Draw her smiling mouth, which is in her belly, and two shapes for her shoes.

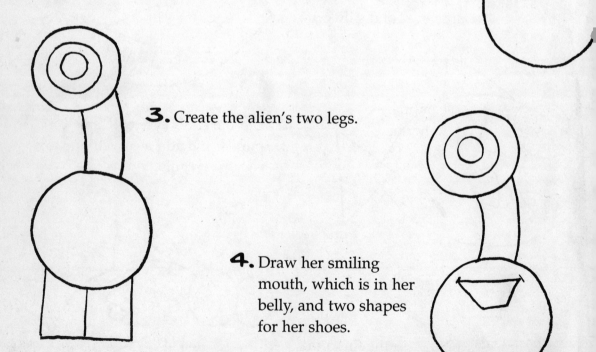

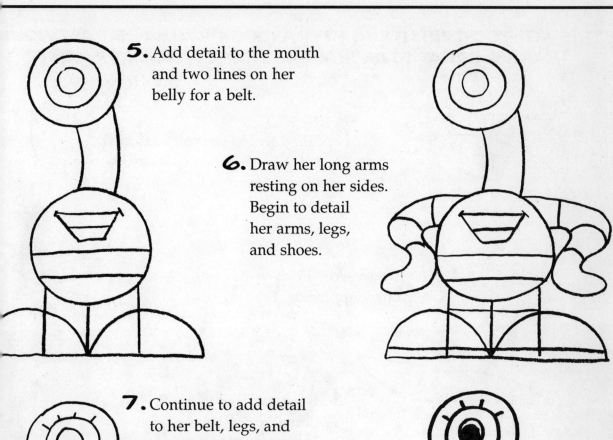

5. Add detail to the mouth and two lines on her belly for a belt.

6. Draw her long arms resting on her sides. Begin to detail her arms, legs, and shoes.

7. Continue to add detail to her belt, legs, and shoes. Sketch eyelashes on her one eye.

8. Erase all uneeded lines. Shade her eye, pants, and mouth as shown. Finish detailing her shoes and clothing.

THIS NOT-TOO-TERRIFYING PTERANODON FROM THE PAST WOUL
MAKE A GREAT STAR IN YOUR NEXT CARTOON DRAWING.

1. Begin drawing the pteranodon's head, a long shape that looks like half of an oval.

2. Then add a second half-oval shape overlapping the first.

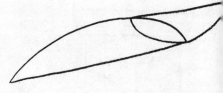

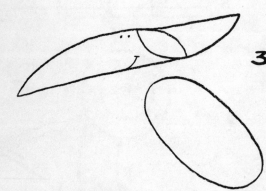

3. Begin to detail the head by drawing small eyes and a mouth. Add this flying reptile's long oval-shaped body.

4. Create its neck, arms, and legs.

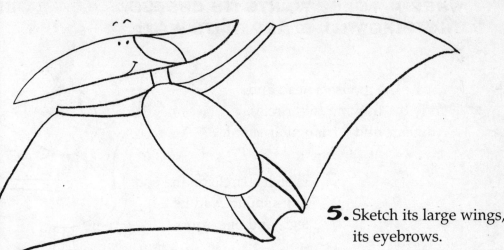

5. Sketch its large wings, as well as its eyebrows.

6. Draw the pteranodon's hands and feet. Erase all unneeded lines, then detail the body and wings.

Mouse and Its Chow

WHEN A MOUSE WANTS ITS CHEESE, NOTHING WILL STAND IN ITS WAY!

1. Create the mouse's head and body by drawing two circles. Add ears and a triangular snout.

2. Sketch a circle on the end of its snout. Add its tail, legs, and one arm.

3. Draw its oval-shaped front paw and its two feet. Detail its head by sketching its eyes and the inner part of its ears.

4. Lightly sketch a small smile. Then draw its other arm and a rectangle for the cheese. Attach a small circle to its front paw.

5. Erase all unnecessary lines, and fill in its nose. Finish the cheese, and add a small cheek line to its face.

Copy This Cat

WATCH OUT, HEATHCLIFF AND GARFIELD! HERE COMES THE KOOKIEST CAT AROUND.

1. Begin by drawing a horizontal oval. Add two round shapes for the cat's eyeballs, then sketch a line down the middle of the oval. Add the small triangular nose and two curved lines for its snout. Draw the pupils.

2. Add two pointed ears and a small clump of fur on its head. Sketch the cat's mouth.

3. Begin to add detail to the cat's head. Draw its inner ears, jaw, and tongue, a long scrawny neck, and dots around its nose and mouth.

4. Add a few whiskers and the round body.

5. Sketch the cat's curled tail and two front legs, then add its four feet.

6. To finish, erase all unnecessary lines. Give your cat spots, plaids, or pointed stripes as shown here. Fill in its inner ears, nose, and mouth. Detail the paws.

Don't Rattle Me

SNAKES ARE NOT THE CUDDLIEST OF CREATURES,
BUT THIS LITTLE RATTLER IS CUTE ENOUGH TO SNUGGLE WITH!

1. Begin by drawing a small horizontal oval. Add two half-circles on top for its eyes. Start to sketch its body with a long *L* shape.

2. Add its pupils and nostrils. Then create the first of the snake's coils.

3. Draw another coil, and add a friendly smile.

4. Sketch the snake's forked tongue, and draw one more coil.

5. Create the remaining part of the snake's body, its tail.

6. Draw rattles on the tail, then add small curved lines around the tail and tongue to show movement. Erase the line between the head and neck.

14

ENGUINS ALWAYS APPEAR DRESSED FOR A NIGHT ON THE TOWN, AND THIS PLEASANT PAL IS NO EXCEPTION.

1. Draw a large egg shape with two tiny feet sticking out from the bottom. Add two small circles for the penguin's eyes.

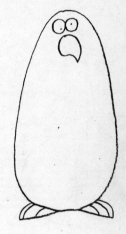

2. Sketch its beak and pupils. Begin to detail the feet.

3. Draw a smaller oval shape within the penguin's body.

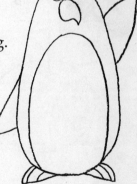

4. Add its flippers, one waving.

5. Detail your penguin by Shading it as shown. Add finishing touches to the feet.

Goofy Google Bird

HAVE YOU EVER MET A GOOGLE BIRD? WELL, THIS ONE'S IRRESISTIBLY SILLY!

1. Draw the google bird's round head, long neck, and large circular body.

2. Add two big eyes and a long, thin rectangle for its front leg.

3. Sketch its beak, its foot, and a curved shape on its belly.

4. Add three large feathers on its head.

5. Continue to "feather" your friend with some on the tail. Draw pupils in its eyes.

6. Now add three small feathers on its side for its wing. Draw part of the second leg and foot. Begin to detail the front foot.

7. Erase all unneeded lines. Darken the far leg and foot, and detail the front leg, foot, and all the feathers. If you have crayons or markers handy, you may want to color in your google bird.

Puffed-Up Puffer

WHEN PUFFER FISH BECOME FRIGHTENED, THEY PUFF UP LIKE A BALLOON. BUT THIS SILLY FISH DOES IT JUST FOR KICKS.

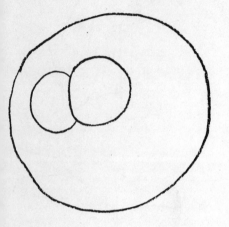

1. Draw a big circle with two eyes inside it.

2. Add cockeyed pupils and a little fishy mouth. Sketch fins on either side.

3. Continue adding fins, and begin to detail its body with small *V*-shaped bumps.

4. Erase extra lines between the bumps and the edge around the body. Finish detailing its body, then add several little air bubbles above its head.

Woolie

HOW MUCH WOOL WOULD A SHY SHEEP SHED IF A SHY SHEEP COULD SHED WOOL?

1. Begin by drawing this woolly sheep's eyes. Underneath them, sketch its snout.

2. Add ears on either side of its eyes. Sketch pupils and a small nose on the end of its snout.

3. Now create its body—a big fluffy one.

4. Draw its legs and small hooves.

5. Erase all unneeded lines, then detail your sheep. Blacken the areas shown, and add a little tuft of wool above the two rear legs.

In Search of Peanuts

THIS POOR ELEPHANT HAS BEEN ON THE HUNT FOR FOOD FOR A LONG TIME! HELP IT OUT BY DRAWING A BURGER DRIVE-THRU OR A BIG JAR OF PEANUT BUTTER.

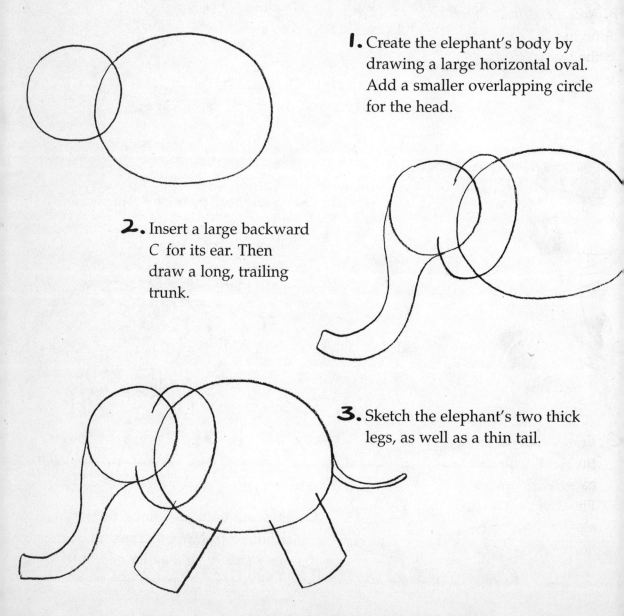

1. Create the elephant's body by drawing a large horizontal oval. Add a smaller overlapping circle for the head.

2. Insert a large backward C for its ear. Then draw a long, trailing trunk.

3. Sketch the elephant's two thick legs, as well as a thin tail.

. Add a little tuft of fur on its tail. Then draw the two sharp tusks.

5. Sketch its other two legs and its eye.

6. Erase all unneeded lines, then detail the eyes, ears, trunk, and tail tuft. Finally, add the elephant's toenails.

Prickles

**PRICKLES THE PORCUPINE IS SWEET TO MEET . . .
UNTIL YOU TRY TO SHAKE ITS PAW.**

1. Draw a large circle for the porcupine's body, overlapped by a smaller circle for its head.

2. Add a snout and ears.

3. Now sketch its feet. On its head, draw the nose and eyes.

4. Add pupils, and begin to create the porcupine's sharp quills.

5. Erase all unneeded lines. Fill in the nose, and detail the paws. Finish by adding lots and lots of sharp quills to your porcupine.

Speedy Sub

BETCHA THIS IS THE GOOFIEST SUBMARINE YOU'LL EVER SEE!

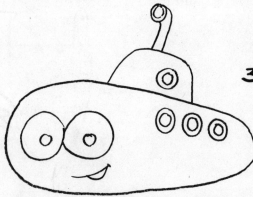

1. Draw a large rounded shape, and give it two big eyes.

2. Add a small grin under the eyes and another rounded shape on top of the submarine.

3. Add four windows and a periscope sticking up from the sub. Draw large pupils in the eyes.

4. Complete your sub by filling in the pupils and mouth, and adding dark shading around the windows. Draw a few posts next to the periscope. Lightly sketch some slightly curved lines to give your sub a rounded look. Finally, add some water and bubbles at the rear of the sub.

My Meerkat

MEERKATS OFTEN STAND ON THEIR HIND FEET TO WATCH FOR ATTACKING BIRDS. THIS LITTLE CREATURE IS JUST CHECKING OUT WHAT ELSE YOU'VE DRAWN!

1. To begin your meerkat, draw a circle for its head and a long oval shape for its body.

2. Connect the two shapes, then add forelegs and a snout.

3. Sketch its hind legs and ears.

4. Add rounded shapes for its paws, a tail, eyes, and eyebrows.

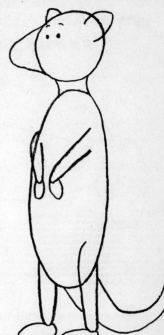

5. Add detail to its head and face, including its inner front ear, nose, and mouth. Draw an underbelly and claw lines on its paws.

6. Finish your meerkat by erasing all unneeded lines. Fill in its nose.

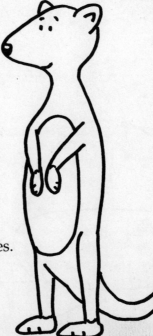

Delightful Dimetrodon

AFTER YOU COMPLETE THIS ONE, YOU CAN CREATE A WHOLE FAMILY OF ADORABLE DIMETRODON DINOSAURS.

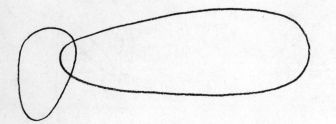

1. Create the head and body by drawing a large horizontal oval, with a smaller vertical oval overlapping it.

2. Add a curved tail, and sketch eyes and eyebrows on its face.

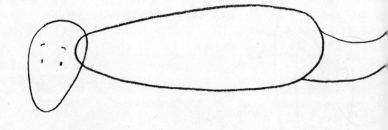

3. Draw the outline for the large frill on the dimetrodon's back. Create outlines for its four legs.

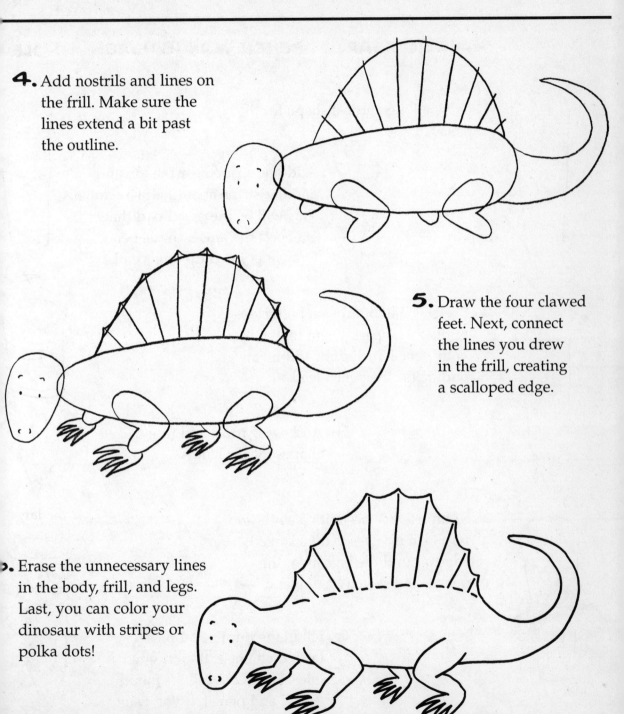

4. Add nostrils and lines on the frill. Make sure the lines extend a bit past the outline.

5. Draw the four clawed feet. Next, connect the lines you drew in the frill, creating a scalloped edge.

6. Erase the unnecessary lines in the body, frill, and legs. Last, you can color your dinosaur with stripes or polka dots!

Pencil Man

HAVE NO FEAR . . . PENCIL MAN IS HERE!

1. Draw a long vertical shape for the pencil.

2. Add one stripe near the top and another stripe about halfway down. This will be the metal part that connects the eraser to the pencil. Draw a pointed tip on its end.

3. Sketch small bumps on both sides of the metal part. Begin to detail your pencil, including adding an outline for the pencil lead.

4. Add eyes, arms, and round shapes for his hands.

5. Complete his face with a smile and pupils in his eyes. Add a jagged edge around the bottom of the pencil, and sketch his fingers.

6. Fill in the pupils and pencil lead, then erase all unneeded lines. Further detail his mouth, eraser, and pencil. If you want, add a wavy pencil line.

THIS CRAZY CAR MAY BE FUN TO DRAW, BUT DRIVING IT COULD BE DISASTROUS.

1. To draw the car, first sketch a half-circle with the straight edge along the bottom. Add two wheels.

2. On the top of the car, draw a square shape, which will be the opening for the convertible seat. Give the car front and back bumpers.

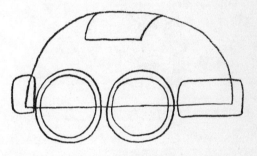

3. Draw hubcaps on the wheels and headlights on the front. Also, outline the grill, which sits on top of the front bumper.

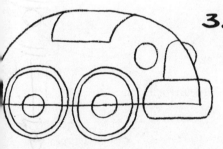

4. Begin to detail the seat, and add a windshield. Sketch eyes with pupils in the headlights, and draw the far wheels.

5. Color in the wheels and pupils. Erase all unnecessary lines. Draw vertical lines on the grill and car seat. Finish the windshield, give the headlights eyebrows, and add a little chugging smoke from the rear of the car.

Cool Clown

DRAW THE CARTOONY CLOWN FACE, THEN CREATE YOUR OWN WACKY BODY FOR IT!

1. Draw a large circle with a smaller circle—the clown's nose—in the center. Add two ears.

2. Insert two huge eyes attached to the nose.

3. Sketch a large grin, a triangle for the hat, and a crescent shape in the nose (to make it look more rounded).

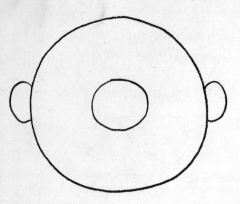

4. Now draw tiny pupils and an outline around the mouth, which touches the clown's nose.

5. Add stars to the hat and teeth to the goofy grin.

6. Give your clown more pizzazz with crazy hair. With short strokes, add lines around the eyes and a tassle to the tip of the hat.

7. Erase the unneeded lines in the mouth. Fill in the nose, hat, and mouth. Shade the hair any way you wish.

Club-Carrying Caveman

DRAW ME. (HE DOESN'T SAY MUCH.)

1. First, draw two overlapping circles, one on top of the other.

2. Begin to detail the caveman's facial features by drawing eyes and eyebrows. Add a large egg shape for his big body.

3. Continue to detail the face, adding a nose, mouth, and ears. Draw an outline for this caveman's clothing—a tiger skin.

4. Add his large feet, and sketch his toes and ankles.

5. Draw the caveman's arms with two circles on the ends for his hands.

6. Put a club in one of his hands, and start to decorate this caveman's clothing.

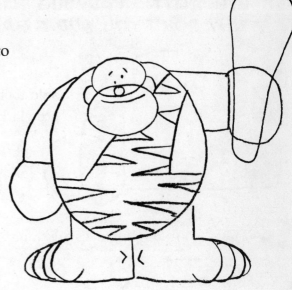

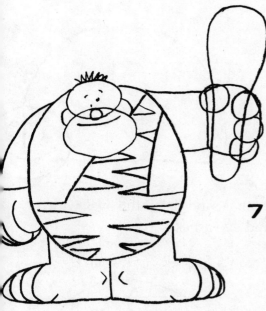

7. Add a small tuft of hair on his head, and sketch his finger shapes.

8. To finish the caveman, erase all unneeded lines. Color in his hair and clothes, and give his club detail. Like most cavemen, this one is hairy! Add small hairs all over his body, toes, fingers, and chin!

Flirty Ladybug

THIS LITTLE LADYBUG FLIES FROM FLOWER TO FLOWER. WHY DON'T YOU ADD A GARDEN BACKGROUND FOR HER?

1. Draw a semicircle with the flat edge along the bottom. Add a circle in the lower right-hand corner for this little ladybug's head.

2. Give your ladybug eyes and a happy smile.

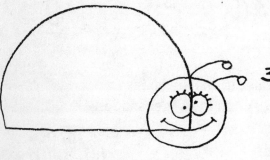

3. Add antennae, and detail the eyes with pupils and eyelashes.

4. Draw spots on her back, then add her five legs (the sixth is hidden behind her head).

5. Erase the unneeded lines in her face. Last, color in her spots and legs.

**THIS SEA SERPENT COMES FROM THE DEEP . . .
THE DEEP END OF A SWIMMING POOL!**

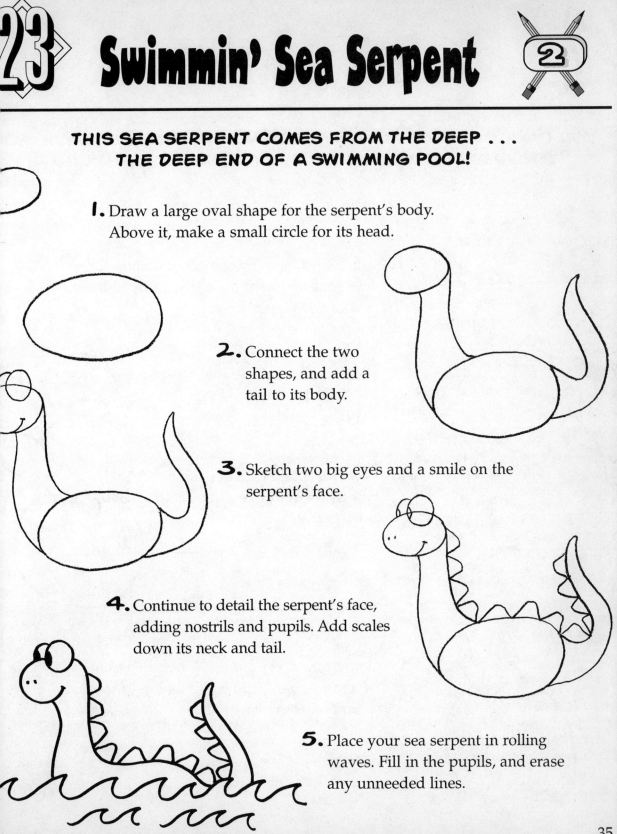

1. Draw a large oval shape for the serpent's body. Above it, make a small circle for its head.

2. Connect the two shapes, and add a tail to its body.

3. Sketch two big eyes and a smile on the serpent's face.

4. Continue to detail the serpent's face, adding nostrils and pupils. Add scales down its neck and tail.

5. Place your sea serpent in rolling waves. Fill in the pupils, and erase any unneeded lines.

Generic Snow Person

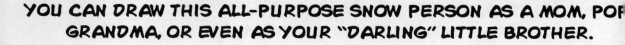

YOU CAN DRAW THIS ALL-PURPOSE SNOW PERSON AS A MOM, POP, GRANDMA, OR EVEN AS YOUR "DARLING" LITTLE BROTHER.

1. Begin with a basic snow person shape—three circles, one on top of the other. Next, add arms and a carrot-shaped nose.

2. Draw two round eyes and a big smile made from five smaller circles.

3. Add buttons down the snow person's front and a thin rectangle tilted on its head for the base of its top hat.

4. Complete the snow person's hat and rest a broom against its arm.

5. Detail the carrot nose and base of the broom. Add a ground line.

6. Erase all unneeded lines, then shade the hat, eyes, mouth, and buttons. Add final details to the broom.

Too-Cute Teddy Bear

FROM THE BERENSTAIN BEARS TO GOLDILOCKS AND HER THREE BEARS, BEARS ARE ALWAYS IN STYLE. (AND THEY'RE "BEAR-Y" FUN TO DRAW!)

1. Draw a large circle for the teddy bear's body, overlapped by a smaller circle for its head. Add two squarish shapes for the arms and a small triangle nose.

2. Add legs and ears. Sketch an upside-down arc for its snout.

3. Draw the teddy bear's button eyes and two small lines extending from its nose to show its mouth.

4. Sketch the teddy bear's bow tie and begin to draw its vest.

5. Finish drawing the outline of the vest. Put in a line at the end of each arm and leg to suggest its paws. Add pockets on the vest.

6. Erase all unneeded lines. Shade the bottom of the nose and the bow tie. Finally, add stripes to the vest.

HAVE YOU EVER MET A SCIENTIST AS MAD AS MORT?

1. Draw an upside-down teardrop shape for the scientist's large head. Add his ears and a small round nose.

2. Begin to create his eyes above his nose, and draw an upturned mouth, slightly smiling.

3. Add wrinkle lines on his forehead, as well as two small eyebrows. Complete his eyes.

4. Sketch a square to create his body.

5. Add the scientist's neck, sleeves, and arms, then begin his feet.

6. Add circular outlines for his hands. Sketch a line down the center of his body from his chin to his feet.

7. Draw four small circles in each hand for fingers. Then, in each hand, place a test tube. Insert tiny buttons down his lab coat.

8. Finally, erase the unneeded lines in his hands, and add details to his shoes. Shade his eyes and the test tubes, and create bubbles coming up from them.

Don't Ruffle Me

THIS REGAL EAGLE PREFERS TO BE DRAWN WITH RED, WHITE, AND BLUE FEATHERS.

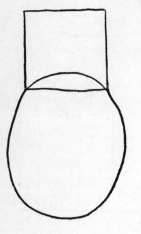

1. First, draw a square for the eagle's head and an overlapping egg shape for its body.

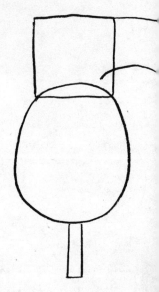

2. Add a large hooked beak, as well as a thin rectangle for its front leg.

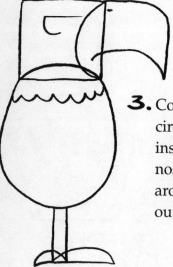

3. Complete its beak with a half-circle. Begin to detail its head, inserting an eye and a small nostril. Add a feathered ruffle around its neck, and sketch the outline of its front foot.

4. Add a pupil, and begin to draw its large wing.

5. Add several more feathers and insert curved lines to suggest the claws on its foot.

6. Draw the eagle's left leg.

7. Erase all unneeded lines. Fill in the eagle's eye, and insert feather lines on its underside. Detail the eagle's legs and claws.

My Zebra Is Zany

NO ZEBRA'S STRIPES ARE ALIKE, SO EACH TIME YOU DRAW THIS CRAZY CREATURE, MAKE SURE ITS STRIPES ARE DIFFERENT.

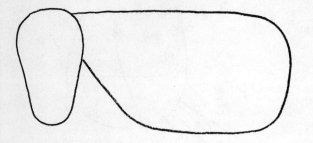

1. Begin by drawing rounded shapes for the zebra's head and body.

2. Begin to detail its body by sketching ears and a thin tail.

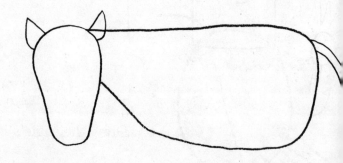

3. Insert two large eyes, and begin to draw its legs.

4. Put in two cockeyed pupils, and draw two curved lines for its nostrils. Add a tuft of hair on the end of its tail, and give your zebra hooves.

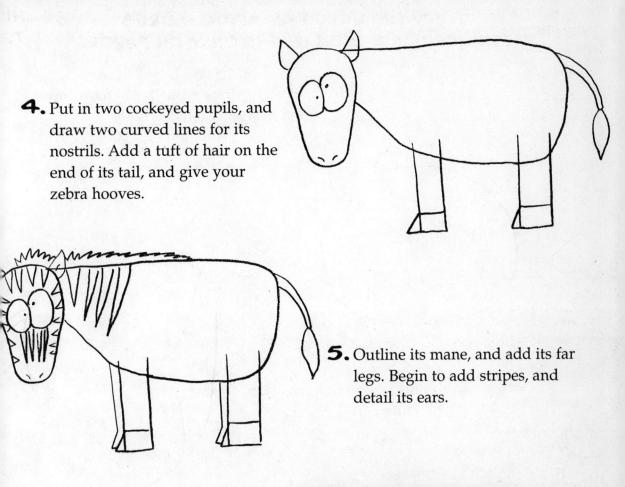

5. Outline its mane, and add its far legs. Begin to add stripes, and detail its ears.

6. Finish drawing the stripes, then erase all unnecessary lines. Fill in the zebra's mane, stripes, and hooves, and detail your zebra's tail tuft.

Pal Apatosaurus

**EVERYONE NEEDS AN APATOSAURUS
FOR A FRIEND, EVEN IF IT IS ONLY ON PAPER.**

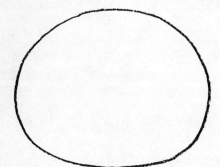

1. To begin, draw a small oval for its head and a large oval for its body.

2. Connect the two shapes with a slightly curving neck.

3. Add the apatosaurus's eyes and two near legs.

4. Draw the visible parts of the two far legs, and put small pupils in its eyes.

5. Give your apatosaurus a smile. Next, add small triangles for its toes, and draw a large curved tail.

6. Erase the lines you don't need in the head, neck, body, and legs.

Artful Aardvark

AARDVARKS ARE UNUSUAL ANIMALS, AND THIS ONE IS AS SILLY AS ANY.

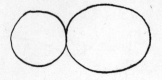

1. Draw a circle and an oval side by side. The oval should be slightly larger than the circle.

2. Add a large long nose to the end of the circle, which is the head. Sketch a tail on the other end.

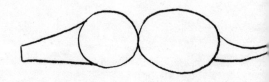

3. Give your aardvark long ears.

4. Add detail to the ears, and draw part of its eye. Sketch its four legs, and add two short lines for toes on its most visible legs.

5. Add an eyeball and a very long tongue to he it catch food. Color in the two far legs, and erase all unnecessary lines.

An Egg on the Way

WHICH CAME FIRST: THE CHICKEN OR THE EGG? THIS LITTLE BIRD SQUAWKS, "THE CHICKEN!"

1. Draw a small circle resting on top of a large, slightly squashed circle. This creates the hen's head and body.

2. Add the hen's beak and goofy eyes.

3. Insert feathers on top of and underneath her head.

4. Give the hen wings and tail feathers. On the beak, add two small nostrils.

5. Erase the lines you don't need in the wings and head. Add straw where your hen can lay plenty of eggs.

EVERYBODY NEEDS A FIDO FOR A FRIEND.

I. For the head and body of this crazy canine, draw two long oval shapes with just a little space between them.

2. Connect the two shapes. The top oval is Fido's head, and the lower one is its body. Add a large nose to its head.

3. Give Fido floppy ears, and add its small eyes.

4. Between its ears, add a little tuft of fur. Add its two near legs and a tail. Don't forget to add a silly smile.

5. Put in circular shapes as outlines for its feet. Sketch motion lines on either side of its tail.

6. Add Fido's far feet, and insert the claws on the two near feet. Draw Fido's food bowl.

7. Erase all unneeded lines, and shade Fido's tail, the ground, and the inside of the bowl. Decorate Fido's food bowl as you like.

On the Lookout

**THIS VULTURE WON'T FLASH HIS FRIENDLY GRIN FOR ANYONE.
(BUT YOU CAN ADD ONE TO HIM IF YOU WANT!)**

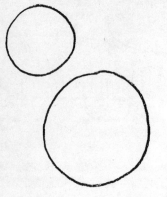

1. To begin, draw the vulture's round head and body.

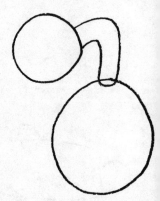

2. Connect the two shapes with a thin curved neck.

3. Add a large hooked beak.

4. Put ruffled feathers around its neck, and sketch its two thin bird legs.

5. Draw its two wings, and add an eye and a nostril.

6. Add six long claws to its legs, and insert a tree branch on which the vulture can rest.

7. Begin to shade the lower portion of its body, including its legs and claws.

8. Complete the shading, and then erase all unneeded lines. Last, add detail to the tree branch.

FOR ADDED FUN, DRAW THIS ODD OCTOPUS IN AN UNDERWATER SETTING WITH GROWING SEAWEED, CRAZY CRABS, AND PLENTY OF FISHIES.

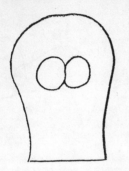

1. Draw the octopus's large head, which also is the base for its legs. Add two big eyes.

2. Sketch its first two legs as shown. Add tiny pupils and a thin mouth.

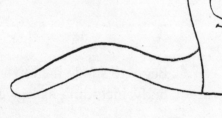

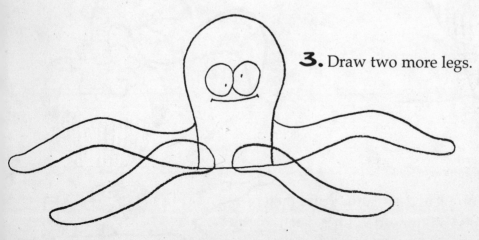

3. Draw two more legs.

Sketch its four back legs.

5. Erase all unneeded lines. Last, add suckers to the bottoms of the front four legs. (The suckers on the back legs are hidden from view.)

Care for a Spin?

THIS CUTE LITTLE ARACHNID WOULD LOVE TO SPIN A WEB FOR YOU!

1. Draw a circle for the spider's head. Add two large eyes. Then, above the head, draw a rounded shape for its body.

2. Detail the spider's face with googly pupils in its eyes and a wide, openmouthed grin. Sketch its four front legs.

3. Add its four back legs.

4. Begin to draw the spider's web with lines stemming straight out from the spider.

5. Start connecting the lines of the web with short curved lines.

6. Complete the web. Darken and shade your spider, but be sure to leave some of its edges white.

Three Wishes

WATCH WHAT YOU WISH FOR . . . THIS JOLLY GENIE MAY GRANT IT!

I. Draw a circle for the genie's head. On top of it, draw its turban, which is a larger rounded shape overlapping the head.

2. Below the genie's head, draw a large round body. Sketch the genie's eyes, nose, and ears. Add a jewel on the turban.

3. Continue to detail its face, drawing pupils and a friendly smile. Begin to add lines in the turban.

4. Create the genie's outstretched arms. Next, further detail the turban, and give the genie a thick mustache.

5. Give the genie hands and a tail-like shape on the end of its body. Finish detailing the turban, and draw the outline of its beard.

6. Dress your genie with a vest and cuffs. Sketch its fingers.

7. Darken the genie's mustache and beard, as well as the jewel in its turban. Decorate its vest, and add final details to its base. Insert smoke, then erase unneeded lines.

Happy Whale

YOU CAN WHIP UP A DRAWING OF THIS WONDERFUL WHALE IN A FLASH.

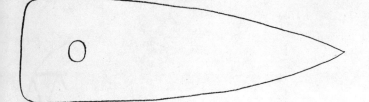

1. Draw a large bullet shape—the pointed end is the whale's tail. Add a small egg shape for the eye.

2. Sketch a horizontal line in the eye for its eyelid. Add a content smile.

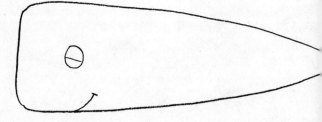

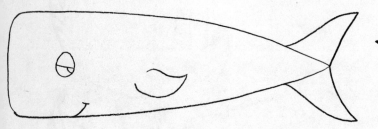

3. Add the pupil, and give your whale its tail and side fins.

4. Erase the extra lines in the tail, darken the pupil, and add water spurting from its spout.

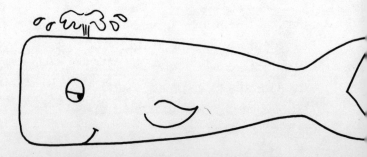

THIS INDIAN BRAVE IS ON THE LOOKOUT FOR A FEW FRESH FEATHERS TO STICK IN HIS HEADBAND!

1. Draw an oval for the brave's head, then add a headband. Decorate the band with a pointed zigzag line. Give your Indian a nose and ears.

2. Start to draw his eyes, and add two lines to create a straight mouth.

3. Put three feathers in his headband. Continue to detail his face with eyebrows, pupils, and face paint.

4. Give your Indian a neck, then detail the feathers and headband. Last, fill in his hair and his pupils.

Somewhere in Space

**FOR YOUR NEXT SCI-FI PICTURE,
INCLUDE THIS HAPPY-GO-LUCKY ASTRONAUT.**

1. Draw a small circle for your astronaut's head. Around it, sketch a larger circle for his space helmet.

2. Under the helmet, draw a square for his space suit. Connect the head to the suit with a short neck. Begin to detail the face with eyes, nose, eyebrows, and ears.

3. Give your astronaut a smile, and add the rectangle-shaped space suit arms.

4. Draw the astronaut's legs, and give him a curly hairdo.

5. Add feet and hands. Then draw cuffs around the wrists, ankles, and waist. Add a thin line between the helmet and space suit. To connect your astronaut to an air supply, put an airhole on the chest of his suit.

6. Further render the space suit with thin lines as shown. Draw a tube coming down from the airhole on the suit.

7. Add connecting pieces between the helmet and suit, then erase the unneeded lines in the air tube. Detail your astronaut with fun patches, buttons, and other decorations on his suit. Add curved lines on the hands and feet, and a small square in the upper right-hand corner of the helmet—these lines make him appear more three-dimensional. Color in the background and his curly hair.

My Moose

DOESN'T EVERYONE NEED
A MOOSE OF HIS OR HER OWN?

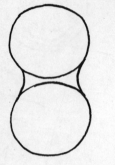

1. Draw two equal-sized circles, one on top of the other. Connect the circles with short curved lines. This will be the moose's face.

2. Add large eyes in the upper circle and two small nostrils below.

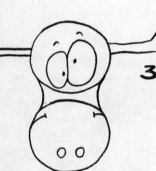

3. Insert pupils, eyebrows, and a grin— only the edges are seen on either side of its face. Now sketch its wide antlers.

4. Add four prongs to its antlers. Sketch a large circle for its body.

5. Add two more prongs to the antlers. Draw the four legs with hooves.

6. Erase all unneeded lines. Fill in the nostrils and hooves. Finally, with short strokes, shade around the moose's head, body, and legs.

65

The Littlest Angel

THIS ANGELIC CREATURE LOOKS ADORABLE ON A HANDMADE CARD FOR A SPECIAL FRIEND.

1. Draw two round shapes, one smaller than the other. This will be the angel's head and body.

2. Add the angel's facial features—eyes, nose, mouth, and ear.

3. Give your angel a thick head of hair, and begin to draw his arm.

4. Add fingers and a thumb to his hand, and insert his two legs.

5. Sketch his toes, and draw his little angelic wrap.

6. Create your angel's characteristic wings and halo.

7. Erase all the lines you don't need. Detail the wings, and add motion lines around them. Make the halo look like it's sparkling with short lines stemming from it. Don't forget to suggest the angel's belly button.

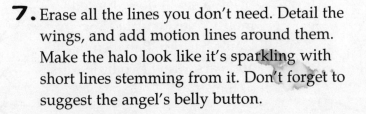

Cowboy Dan

COWBOY DAN LOVES HORSIN' AROUND. PUT HIM ON A BUCKIN' BRONCO OR A REAL ANGRY STEER.

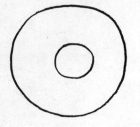

1. Draw a large circle for Dan's head and a smaller circle for his nose.

2. Above his nose, sketch lines for his squinty eyes. Add a large curlicue mustache and ears.

3. Insert a small downturned mouth. Next, create Cowboy Dan's hat rim. Between his hat and ears, draw two little tufts of hair.

4. Finish his hat by adding its top. Sketch a triangle under his chin for his neckerchief.

5. Draw a thick neck to connect the neckerchief to his head. Add a knot to the neckerchief. On his hat, draw a wide band.

6. Decorate the band with ovals or however you wish. Shade his hair and mustache, and detail his neckerchief.

Go, Snail, Go!

THIS SNAIL IS NO SLOWPOKE!
YOU CAN DRAW IT IN A FEW SIMPLE STEPS.

1. Draw a large rounded shape with a flat bottom edge for the snail's body. To its left, draw a small circle for the head.

2. Connect the head to the body with curved lines, and add a tail. Sketch antennae, eyes, and a mouth.

3. Add small bulbs on the ends of the antennae. Connect the neck and tail to the shell with two thin shapes.

4. Erase all the lines you don't need, and add a spiral shape to decorate the shell.

Smilin' Smilodon

THIS SMILODON HAS HUGE FRONT TEETH— THE BETTER TO EAT A CHEESEBURGER WITH, MY DEAR!

1. To draw the head of the smilodon, first sketch a large circle. Next, draw a small triangle inside for its nose.

2. Add two rounded shapes for its cheeks, and create its eyes and ears.

3. Put in eyebrows, whiskers, and a tongue, then sketch its large teeth.

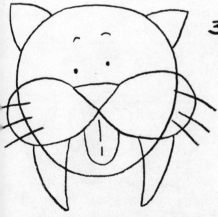

4. Detail the ears, and add a little tuft of hair on top of its head. Erase all the lines you don't need, and fill in the smilodon's nose.

Dopey Dirk

**AFTER YOU DRAW THIS SILLY LITTLE MAN,
COLOR HIM IN BRIGHT FLUORESCENT SHADES!**

1. Draw a large circle for Dirk's head and a smaller circle for his nose.

2. Now insert another circle for his body. Put a line through its center for a waistline. Add ears.

3. Continue to detail his face with eyes and a mouth.

4. Put pupils in the eyes, and draw a goofy tongue coming from his mouth. Next, add his outstretched arms.

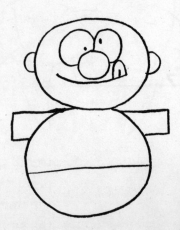

5. Draw the circular outlines of his hands. Add his feet, and place a beanie cap atop his head.

6. Detail the beanie with a small propeller. Add curly hair, and sketch Dirk's stubby fingers. Give Dirk some suspenders.

7. To detail Dirk, decorate his pants, shirt, and suspenders as you wish. Add thin soles on the bottom of his feet to create shoes, and a few lines on his beanie. Further render his hands, and erase the unneeded lines in his fingers.

Oink!

YOU CAN CREATE ALL SORTS OF CORNY CARTOONS WITH THIS LITTLE PORKER.

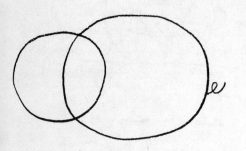

I. Draw a large round shape for this oinker's big body. Add an overlapping circle for its head and a curlicue tail on the other end.

2. Detail its face with eyes, a nose, and ears. Add its four squatty legs.

3. Add pupils in the eyes and nostrils in the nose. Give your pig a big wide smile. Insert lines for hooves on its feet.

4. Fill in its pupils and nostrils. Erase all unneeded lines.

Traveling Turtle

SO WHERE IS THIS TURTLE HEADING? ONLY YOU KNOW!

1. Draw a rounded oblong shape that is flattened on the bottom. This will be the turtle's shell. Then insert a thin stripe running across the lower part of the shell.

2. On the lower section, draw a few vertical lines running across the bottom. Add the turtle's head and tail.

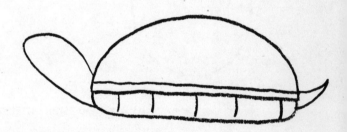

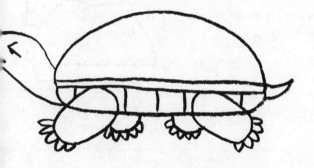

3. Create its four legs and toes. Sketch the facial features: an eye, an eyelid, and a mouth.

4. To detail your turtle, first erase the unneeded lines. Next, add scaly skin to its legs and a crisscross pattern to its shell. Add a shadow underneath your turtle, and place him on dry, pebbled ground.

Karate Kal

YOU BETTER HOPE KARATE KAL IS YOUR PAL!

1. Draw two circles, the smaller one for Kal's head and the larger one for his body.

2. Add a karate belt around his waist and a headband around his forehead. Add ears and a nose, and begin to sketch his eyes.

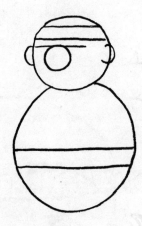

3. Sketch the wild hair on his head. Complete his eyes, and insert a wide, open mouth. Create his arms and legs.

4. Add the circular outlines for his feet and hands. Begin to draw his karate clothes, called a *gi* (pronounced GEE).

5. Continue to draw his *gi*, including cuff lines around his wrists and ankles, and add a belt. Next, add fingers and toes.

6. Finish Karate Kal by coloring in his belt, hair, eyes, and mouth. Erase the lines you don't need, and further render his toes and fingers.

Joe Hollywood

JOE HAS ALWAYS WANTED TO BE A STAR, BUT YOUR DRAWING I
PROBABLY THE MOST FAMOUS HE'LL EVER BE!

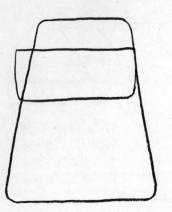

1. For Joe's head, draw a four-sided shape with rounded corners. Across the eye area, draw a rectangle. This will be the guide for his supercool shades.

2. Begin to detail his sunglasses by outlining the frames on the sides and top. Draw Joe's nose.

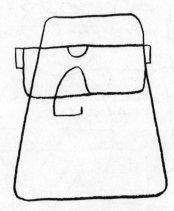

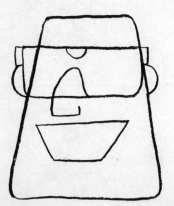

3. Add his ears and a wide grin.

4. Sketch Joe's thick hair. Add a small line for his chin and one on either side of his mouth.

5. Insert lines for his teeth, and add more hair below his ears. Draw a *V*-neck shirt and collar, and add a small line under his mouth for the dimple in his chin. Put two thin rectangles in his glasses.

6. Add lines for his shoulders, then erase the lines you don't need. Shade his glasses, leaving the two rectangles blank. Last, color under his mouth and around his neck and shirt collar.

Dragon Baby

THIS LITTLE DRAGON CAN FIRE UP
ANY FUN PICTURE.

1. Draw one circle for its head and a smaller overlapping circle for its snout.

2. Add a mouth in the smaller circle and eyes in the larger one. On top of the baby's head, sketch the ears.

3. Give the dragon baby a big round body. Next, sketch teeth and nostrils on its snout. Add eyebrows above its eyes.

4. Draw round, stubby arms and feet. Add little claws to its feet and scalloped wings behind its arms.

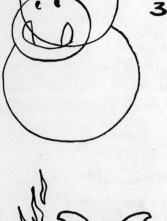

5. Erase the lines you don't need. Insert foot pads on th bottoms of its feet and arm cuffs around the wrists. Add an oval for the tummy—its soft spot—and detai the wings. Finally, add a few little flames coming up from the dragon's nostrils.

'1135